# The Bible Battle

### Karl Keating

RASSELAS
HOUSE

Published by Rasselas House
El Cajon, California
RasselasHouse.com

Cover design by EbookLaunch.com
Formatting by PolgarusStudio.com

ISBN 978-1-942596-21-9 Paperback
ISBN 978-1-942596-20-2 Ebook

# Contents

# Introduction

If any of my debate opponents could be called a "character," it was Peter S. Ruckman. He styled himself a Fundamentalist, but most Fundamentalist writers disavowed him, partly for his singular beliefs but mostly for his acerbic personality. Even when other Fundamentalists thought Ruckman was right in his ideas, they usually thought he was wrong in his attitudes and approach, doing their cause more harm than good.

I was invited to debate Ruckman as the final event in a weeklong Bible conference. The topic was whether the Catholic religion is true. The venue was the First Baptist Church of Long Beach, California, the city in which I grew up. More than 400 people attended, the large majority of them conference attendees or other Fundamentalists, but there were some Catholics present.

All I knew about Ruckman was that he was the pastor of a church in Pensacola, Florida. I had tried locating his books—I had been told he had written several—but was unsuccessful. By a happy chance, the day before the debate someone sent me two copies of his monthly, the *Bible Believers' Bulletin*. From the letters column, which included pleas to remove the correspondents' names from the mailing list, I took it that Ruckman's publication was distributed to many people who preferred not to get it. These were not Catholics but other Fundamentalists.

Fundamentalism is by no means monolithic. Ruckman dismissed most fellow Fundamentalists not just as compromisers but as non-Christians, apparently little better than Catholics. He faulted them for using what he regarded as faulty Bibles, anything other than the original, 1611 edition of the King James Version. Indeed, he wrote that "modern Fundamentalists are cockeyed with apostasy." Ruckman, it turned out, was one of the chief proponents of the so-called King James Only school. He maintained that that translation not only was far superior to any other but provided "advanced revelation," a term I never found a good definition of.

I got to the church early and introduced myself to the hosting pastor. Later, in the hallway, he was walking with Ruckman. The pastor introduced us, I said I was pleased to meet Ruckman, and Ruckman gave a harumph. He shook hands but wasted no time in small talk. It was as though he was afraid of catching something from me. This impression was reinforced at the end of the debate—actually, before what was supposed to be the end of the debate— when he went to the podium and said these would be his last remarks. As soon as he finished making his comments, he walked out of the room, leaving me to give my final talk. No handshake, no goodbye.

I wasn't surprised. His attitude during the debate said a lot. Like every professional anti-Catholic, he claimed to like and respect Catholics, but actions do speak louder. Whenever I made a point he found discomfiting, he gave a large, theatrical yawn or held up a placard for the crowd to read. I don't recall what the placard said, but it wasn't in praise of the Catholic position. In this Ruckman was mimicked by a fan of his in the front row. This man had two signs. One, in red lettering, said, "Amen, Brother Ruckman." The other, in black, said "Repent Catholic." The signs alternated, depending on who was at the microphone.

One could spot the Fundamentalists at the debate easily, and not just from the signs. Each came armed with a Bible. Many Catholics had them, too, but the Fundamentalists seemed to wield the Good Book aggressively. Many questions directed to me were of the "How do you square this verse with Catholicism?" type. Clearly, some people had taken pains to prepare themselves to ask just the right question, the one that would throw the Papist for a loop.

Ruckman, like most Fundamentalist speakers, did not debate so much as preach. He flipped through the Bible, instructing the audience to turn first to this verse, then to that one. (Most of his tedious page-turning instructions have been edited out of the transcript.) He asked listeners to read aloud with him. He pumped them for shouted "amens" as though he were a cheerleader at a football game.

It was hard to keep a straight face when he was doing this kind of thing because the tactic worked against him. His rudeness backfired. Dozens of people, Catholics and Fundamentalists alike, came up to me during the breaks and apologized for Ruckman's behavior. I may have made few converts, but it was clear he made none. One woman said to me something like, "Your composure in the face of this hostility speaks well of your religion." I like to think that's how it came across, but no doubt a portion of that "composure" was simple bewilderment at Ruckman's antics.

As I said, Ruckman preached from the Bible—yes, he did thump it a few times—and most adults in the audience had Bibles in their laps. (There were many children present, too, perhaps brought by their parents so they could see that strangest of animals, a believing Catholic.) During a question period, one fellow asked me, "Why didn't you bring a Bible?" I explained that speaking styles differ. I prefer to speak either from memory or from detailed notes that include scriptural quotations. Using notes is more convenient than noisily flipping through the pages of the Bible. As a spectator, I've never liked watching a speaker read from (and get lost in) a book. I think I should know my material well enough that I don't have to impose that annoyance on the crowd.

What's more, I don't like citation-dropping. Sometimes a speaker may need to give chapter and verse, but usually not. If the quotation is "Thou art Peter, and upon this rock I will build my church," a mention of "Matthew 16:18" is nearly useless: if you already know the verse, a citation is unnecessary; if you don't know it, a citation is almost pointless, since it would take you a while to locate the quotation, and by that time the discussion would have turned to a different verse.

However true all this may have be, I took the questioner's complaint into account. Next time I debated I took along a Bible plus my notes. I spoke extemporaneously with some reference to the notes. I placed the opened Bible before me, occasionally and randomly turning the pages, thus pacifying those who looked at Scripture as a talisman, thinking that if you don't touch the sacred pages, you can't say anything intelligent about Christianity.

So that was one lesson I learned. Another and more important one was this: keep calm, don't let the antics of the other speaker or of the audience throw you off. Let's face it. Few people are converted by arguments aired at a single debate. What the Catholic debater wants to do is leave a certain impression. That is usually the most he can hope for. With Fundamentalists, so suspicious of things Catholic, so confused about the Catholic religion, the goal is to leave them with the notions that (a) Catholics do not have fangs, (b) something intelligent, even if not entirely convincing, can be said in favor of the Catholic position, and (c) the Bible has more to say in favor of Catholic beliefs than they imagined.

Another lesson: keep an eye on the literature table. I put several hundred copies of one of my tracts in the foyer. By the lunch break they were all gone, yet I knew few people had picked up copies, since it wasn't until after lunch that I had a chance to mention their availability. Clearly, someone had "liberated" the tracts. But I had come prepared, went to the car, brought in plenty more, and posted a friend at the table.

Given annoyances like these, are debates worthwhile? I think they're absolutely necessary, for three reasons. First, anti-Catholics need to know they'll be called to account in front of their Fundamentalist admirers. In the long run, this can do wonders for their honesty. Second, Fundamentalists need to see Catholics defend their faith. If it isn't worth defending, why should anyone believe in it? Third, Catholics need to learn there are sensible replies to the standard charges. They should rest comfortably knowing the slanders are groundless.

Whether I succeeded in any of that must be left to the reader of these pages.

# Notes on the Text

The following transcript has been edited for clarity and concision. I have taken the liberty of correcting grammatical errors and obvious misstatements, and I have removed those seemingly unavoidable hesitations and starts (ah's and um's and their cousins) that may not be particularly off-putting when spoken but seem to gouge the eyes when in print. The four debates in the series have been made roughly uniform in length. When given publicly, they ranged from two hours to an almost unendurable four hours, counting question-and-answer sessions. Each is now short enough to be read at a single sitting.

I have attempted to retain each speaker's best arguments, feeling no temptation to omit my opponents' most persuasive comments. (I think the Catholic position, however inadequately expressed by me, is match enough for any charge leveled against it.) I have omitted or truncated exchanges that were redundant or seemed unhelpful to the audiences. Also omitted have been audience questions that strayed too far from the topics of the debates or that were not true questions but attempted preaching sessions.

Looking back at my own arguments, particularly those made when on defense, I find places where I could have made a better reply. I have not gussied up my remarks. A reader may say, "But you could have said *this*!" My excuse must be that *this* didn't occur to me at that moment. Perhaps I was taken off guard. Perhaps my mind went blank. Perhaps I just didn't yet know the best answer and could offer only the second-best answer. What is presented here is verisimilitude. I can use a phrase from nineteenth-century German historian Leopold von Ranke. I have attempted to give the story *"wie es eigentlich gewesen"*—"how it really was."

And how it really is today. There is not a single anti-Catholic claim in these books that has fallen out of circulation. The claims have been around for lifetimes, and there is no likelihood that they ever will disappear completely, human nature and human obstinacy being what they are. I have tried to respond to the claims with candor and fairness. Whether I have succeeded is for readers to judge. Throughout the debates I kept in mind that "the truth shall set you free." I always have found searching for truth—and debating what is true—to be exhilarating. I hope you will too, as you read what follows, and I hope these pages bring solace and confidence to Catholics and intrigue and light to non-Catholics.

# Debate Transcript:
# Karl Keating vs. Peter S. Ruckman

MODERATOR: The format that we have decided upon has been agreed upon by the principals. These gentlemen will be exchanging comments at ten-minute intervals. If they go over the ten minutes, it's my job to step up here and say, "Shut up, you're done."

They're going to swap comments and rebuttals for somewhere between 40 and 60 minutes, and then we are going to open it to questions from the floor. I will field the questions. If your question is irrelevant, I will tell you so. You are not a participant in the debate. These two gentlemen are. You are not debating anyone. You will be given the option to ask questions. There is a difference. If you stand up and try to preach a sermon and straighten these gentlemen out, I'll tell you you're out of place, sit down, and be quiet. I've become reasonably proficient at that.

All right, we're giving Mr. Keating the option to open his comments, and whatever introductory comments he has is fine. Whatever subject he'd like to pursue, initially, is fine, and then Dr. Ruckman has said that he would be glad to respond to whatever he has to say. Mr. Keating, the floor is yours, fire away.

KEATING: I'd like to begin with the inspiration of Scripture. As most of you realize, today's event is the culmination of a week-long Bible conference, so it seemed to me I ought to begin with this topic. The question really is, why should the Bible be taken as a rule of faith? Well, because it's inspired, one might say. But how do we know it is inspired? Now there are some inadequate reasons for thinking so.

First is the cultural reason. In our country, we come from a Judeo-Christian heritage. No matter how lax our faith might be, we think that the Bible has a certain official status, and we would not speak about it the way we might speak about the Koran or the works of Confucius. Unfortunately the cultural view of the Bible is not enough to show its inspiration. After all, if you lived in a Muslim country and were brought up there, that kind of argument would demonstrate to you the truth and the inspiration of the Koran, which we know is not inspired.

The second reason one might think the Bible is inspired is family tradition. "I was brought up with it. It was good enough for my ancestors, so it's good enough for me." There is a certain logic to that, but it doesn't prove the inspiration of Scripture.

As a third reason, some people say, "Scripture is so inspirational. I can tell from reading it, it moves me so." "Inspirational" is a word with a double meaning. We use it, in the wider sense, to refer to many different kinds of writing. The problem is that some parts of the Bible are not at all emotionally moving. Some are as dry as military statistics because they are military statistics, such as much of the Book of Numbers. On the other hand, some non-inspired books, such as *The Imitation of Christ* by Thomas à Kempis, are more moving than many whole books of the Bible, yet the *Imitation* is not inspired.

Now we come to a fourth, better argument, the Bible's own claim to inspiration. It's infrequent. In the New Testament, the only writer who seems to have been aware that he was operating under the inspiration of the Holy Spirit was the writer of Revelation. In the Old Testament, several books say that what follows in them is inspired, but most of the books don't. Even if each book of the Bible claimed inspiration, that would not prove the matter because the Koran, the Book of Mormon, and the writings of Mary Baker Eddy, the founder of Christian Science, claim the same thing. That the Bible says it's inspired, at least with respect to some of its books, is not sufficient.

The fifth inadequate reason is the claim that "the Holy Spirit tells me so. I read the Bible, and I receive a conviction that the Bible is inspired, so it must be inspired." Here we fall into subjectivism. The good Muslim is going to say the same thing about the Koran. And someone who is neither a Muslim nor a Christian would have no rational basis for distinguishing from the other.

In the long run, it's only the Catholic position on inspiration that can prove the inspiration of the Bible. This is how the argument works. First we consider the Bible as a non-inspired book, just another ancient manuscript. The first thing we discover is that we have a very reliable manuscript, compared to all the other ancient manuscripts. We have manuscripts going back even to the first and second centuries, many of them. For many ancient writers, the oldest manuscripts we have are ones that were written long after they died. For Livy it's 500 years; for Horace, 900; for Plato, 1,300; for Euripides, 1,600. Nobody argues that we don't have authentic manuscripts from those writers. Thus, from textual criticism we are able to determine that the Bible, as we have it, is accurate as a manuscript.

Then we argue from the historical reliability of the Bible. From what we find in other ancient Christian writings, and from what we know of human nature, we say there is only one solution to the empty tomb, which is that Christ was what he said he was, namely God, and that he rose from the dead. We then find that he said he would do something, which is to found a Church that would continue throughout the ages. That Church must have as one of its notes the note of infallibility. It must be able to teach its doctrines correctly and not defect from them. Seeing that the Church is infallible in its official teaching, we know that when it tells us that the Bible is inspired, we can accept its word.

Note, this is not a circular argument. A circular argument would say, "The Bible says the Church is infallible, and the Church says the Bible is inspired." That's a circular argument. This instead is a spiral argument. The circular argument presupposed inspiration of the Bible. In the Catholic argument, we don't make that presupposition. We begin with the Bible as a regular historical text and then we argue from it to the infallibility of the Church. Once we have that, we listen to the Church that tells us the Bible is, indeed, inspired.

RUCKMAN: In regards to proof for the inspiration of the Bible, we don't assume anything, least of all that something as obtuse as reaching back in the Church Fathers to prove that a church would be the authority. Nothing that obtuse. Our reason for believing the King James Bible is the Word of God and that the Bible was originally given as inspired is not a historical argument or a comparative argument. It's a scientific argument. We think of the Bible as inspired because of mathematical computers. We don't rest by any assumptions at all.

You say what's the proof of this? The Bible says, "Prove all things; hold fast to that which is good." And reading from Isaiah, the Holy Spirit told you how to tell whether or not he was doing the writing or somebody else was. I'm in Isaiah 44:7: "The proof of inspiration is prophecy." He doesn't rest on anything as obtuse as what somebody thinks about their religion. That's immaterial. We're talking about mathematics here.

We know the Bible is inspired because of its mathematical statistics. I have here a book that gives 48 prophecies about a man before he is born, anywhere within 400 to 1,000 years before he was born. All of them come true on the money. We're not dealing with religion at all. We believe the Bible is inspired because of scientific, mathematical, computerized, statistical probability. There isn't any question about it.

Now, if you want to get a computer to work this thing out, you work it out like this. In the Bible, you are told more than 400 years before Christ was born that he would be born in Bethlehem of Judea. You got to figure one chance out of twelve, with twelve tribes, Judah is only one of them. You've got to figure a chance one out of 27. There are 27 towns in Judah. Now you take 48 prophecies and one man and figure what the chances are of 48 prophecies coming to pass, one individual, 400 years before he was born. And those chances, and I'll leave you to your own computer to figure it out, are ten to the hundred and fifty-seventh power. That's ten with a hundred and fifty seven zeros after it. You say how do we know the Bible is inspired? By mathematical, scientific, statistical evidence that can be proved in court. Figure out the probability.

For example, suppose I got up this morning and I said, "In the year 2154 a man is going to be born, in Dothan, Alabama, who lives to be 28 years old and is killed in a traffic accident in downtown Chicago, between Newberry and 12th street, at 1:30 in the afternoon. His funeral will cost $2,154.25. He'll be buried in West Long Cemetery in St. Louis after the body is shipped, and the presiding preacher at the funeral will be Reverend So-and-So." You'd say you're crazy. The computer couldn't handle it. Somebody said it can store up one hundred fifty million facts a second. That won't do at all. This book is 48 prophecies of a man before he was born and all of them came through, on the money.

Finally, I'll say this: we know the Bible is inspired, not because any Catholic said anything. The word "Catholic" doesn't appear in history until 113 A.D. It was invented by a man named Ignatius, a Church Father, not an early Christian of the Bible. No early Christian of the Bible ever referred to any church as the Catholic Church. That's a Greek term. Comes from Ignatius. It's borrowed from Greek philosophy. We wouldn't have to ask any Catholic if that book is inspired. If it wasn't inspired, we wouldn't take his opinion on it if he thought it was.

I'm not accepting the Bible to be inspired because any church told me. I'm accepting it inspired because it proved itself to be so mathematically, and two other things. The Bible says, "He that is of God heareth God's word. If any man will do his will, he shall know the doctrine, whether I speak of myself or whether it be of God."

The brother said it was only in Revelation they talked about inspiration. That's incorrect. In 2 Peter 3, Simon Peter, the prince of apostles, said that Paul wrote Scripture. In 2 Timothy 3:16, Paul said, "All Scripture is given by inspiration of God." Simon Peter said the Pauline epistles were Scripture before the Catholic Church ever showed up.

KEATING: I confess I am somewhat taken aback by the mathematical argument. I never thought I would hear a Christian use an argument that might be used by Carl Sagan, the astronomer, an agnostic.

His argument is that, mathematically, the odds are such that there must be other inhabited planets in the universe. He calculates the number of galaxies, the odds that one star might have planets, the odds that a planet might have an atmosphere, the odds that the atmosphere might have oxygen. He comes to the conclusion that it's a mathematical certainty that there are zillions of other worlds like ours, with human beings on them. I don't put much stock in Carl Sagan's calculations because they don't really prove the matter. In fact, I could mention to you astronomers who have shown that, mathematically, he's just wrong.

I've never had anybody argue the inspiration of the Bible on mathematics. I don't believe that it's a good proof. No matter what statistic you may come up with, it is not 100 percent. You always have a probability—that was Dr. Ruckman's word. There is no disagreement between us as to whether the book of Isaiah is inspired. I accept it. I accept its true prophecy. That's not a problem. But did you notice that the most that can be proved from that argument—let us presume that the argument, in fact, can prove inspiration based on mathematics—the most that can be proved is that the book of Isaiah is inspired because it is a prophetical book? What about the Song of Songs? What about one of the shorter epistles? What about some of the other Old Testament books that don't have any explicit prophecy in them?

You might say, well, if I could prove one book's inspired, the whole Bible is inspired. That doesn't follow because you first have to prove what constitutes the Bible. What books belong to the canon of Scripture? That's the key. The Catholic Church has identified a list of 73 books that it says are inspired and belong in the canon.

Another point you brought up was that the word "Catholic," which means universal, was not used until Ignatius of Antioch used it. Quite true. It's not used for the name of the Church in the Bible. On the other hand, the word "Trinity" is not found in the Bible. We believe in the Trinity. The word "Incarnation" is not found in the Bible. We believe in the Incarnation. We believe in those because they are described in other words in the Bible. The Catholic position is that the existence of the Catholic Church is taught in the Bible, even though the word Catholic Church is not there.

MODERATOR: All right, we'll allow Dr. Ruckman his next time period.

RUCKMAN: I was talking about mathematical possibility that was fulfilled. Past tense. I'm dealing with a case, not where a fellow is going to guess out there, I'm talking about a guess where he found them out there.

Now, the statement was, what about books like the Song of Solomon that don't contain prophecy? I would like sometime, before this meeting is over, and this discussion is over, I would like to see our brother find me one book in the Old Testament that doesn't have any prophecy in it. One will be just fine. He can take Obadiah if he wants to; it only has one chapter. I'll show him, at least, three items in it that are future. There are 39 books in the Old Testament.

I don't know of a single book in the Old Testament that doesn't have a prophetic subject in it. If you ever find one, let me know. I'm not too bright. I've only read the Bible though about 106 times. I may have missed something. But if I've missed it, I certainly missed it somewhere. I can take you to the Song of Solomon and show you the rapture, and the advent, and the Antichrist of the Church, and a dozen other things in there.

Now, in regard to this authentic interpreter, infallible interpreter, fortunately, we have a self-interpreting book. Simon Peter, the prince of apostles says, "No prophecy of the Scripture is of any private interpretation. Holy men of God spaketh and were moved by the Holy Ghost." The interpreter is the Holy Ghost, not some body of people who profess to be the one true Church that Christ founded, which might be true and then again it might not be true.

Luke 24:44: "These the words which I spake unto you while I was yet with you. All things must be fulfilled which were written in the law of Moses and in the prophets and in the psalms concerning me." Watch it, verse 45: "Then opened he their understanding that they might understand the Scripture." The infallible, divine interpreter is the Lord himself. He opened their eyes. No church had any part in that thing at all.

1 Corinthians 2:9: "But as it is written, eye hath not seen nor ear heard neither have entered into the heart of man the things which God hath prepared for them that love him." Watch it, verse 10: "But God hath revealed them unto us by his church." Right? No, that isn't right. Some fellow made that up. God hath revealed them to us by his what?

PEOPLE: Spirit.

RUCKMAN: By his what?

PEOPLE: Spirit.

RUCKMAN: By his what?

PEOPLE: Spirit.

RUCKMAN: One more time.

PEOPLE: Spirit.

RUCKMAN: Louder.

PEOPLE: Spirit!

RUCKMAN: Okay.

KEATING: Maybe I should have brought a cheering section of my own.

You know it's very difficult for anybody who's on the defensive to be able to respond to every potshot. It's much easier to make an accusation than a reply, particularly if the accusation is partly true and partly false. First, you've got to distinguish which is which. Then you've got to explain why the false part is false.

Dr. Ruckman says he's read the Bible 106 times. Well, he's read it more often than I, but it's evident to me, through my lesser number of readings, that the Bible is not self-interpreting. A book cannot interpret itself. It's a mind that interprets, either the mind of the reader or the mind of an authority, like God himself, or the mind of a living Church. A book, by itself, cannot interpret. We need an interpreter.

When we sit down and read the Bible, how do we get the proper interpretation? What it comes down to in most cases is either what we've been brought up with as an interpretation or what our minister or pastor says.

What constitutes the New Testament? Our Lord didn't say. None of the writers said these are the 27 books that make up the New Testament. You do not find anything like that in the Bible. You find no listing of the New Testament books within the books themselves, so how do we know which ones belong?

Now we know that Paul wrote books other than those that appear in the Bible, books that were lost. Presumably other writers wrote other things. Peter must have written other letters during his life but we presume that those lost books were not inspired. How did the early Christians know which were inspired, which were not? The New Testament does not tell us. We need an infallible authority to inform us what constitutes the canon. Without that authority, we can't know what comprises the Bible.

I want to point out that when we say, "the Holy Spirit tells me," what we're really saying is these books move me, that I see religious truth in them. Luther said the proof of inspiration is what? It's the power to convict us of the truth of the Christian message. The problem with Luther's standard is that he could have written a book that could convey the Christian message, but that book would not have been inspired. You could write one sentence that would be true and moving, but it would not be inspired. So we have to find out some other basis for deciding that our four Gospels and the epistles belong to the canon of Scripture.


RUCKMAN: How many of you people here were Catholic before you were born-again, you received Christ and left the Catholic Church? Would you stand. Would you stand. I'll stand with you. All right, thank you. Be seated. I have here *A Catechism for Adults* by Rev. William J. Clogan. Nothing objectionable. Imprimatur by the archbishop of Chicago. There it is. This is since Vatican II. Vatican II won't cover up this work. This is 1972, a catechism for adults. I'm an adult. I want to know what Catholics believe.

When I went to school, they taught reading, writing, and arithmetic, and we learned how to read. So I read on page 54, "Has the Catholic Church ever changed its teaching? Answer, no. For 2,000 years the Church has taught the same things which Jesus Christ taught." What I think a Catholic teaches is immaterial. I want it from the horse's mouth.

Now regard to the Holy Spirit leading people. I want to call your attention, very quickly, to about three items. In Acts 11:24, Barnabas is said to be a good man filled with the Holy Ghost. Acts 11:24. And that fellow, good man, filled with the Holy Ghost, who was around before Ignatius, knew what the word "Catholic" meant. That fellow got into an argument with Paul, who was the most Spirit-filled apostle in the New Testament. In Acts 15:39 there are two Spirit-filled, born-again men that don't agree, and the Holy Spirit is leading both of them. The contention was so sharp between them, they departed asunder, and Barnabas took Mark one way and Paul took Silas the other. You see that? Both those men were filled with the Holy Ghost. The Lord leads one bunch this way, other bunch that way, and they're both filled with the Holy Ghost.

Our brother says how are you going to know what's right? How are you going to prove all things? John 16:13: "when the Holy Spirit is come, he will guide you and lead you into all truth." Now, he didn't say you'd accept it, but he said he'd guide you. He didn't say you'd believe it, but he said he'd teach it to you. The fact that some Christians reject what the Holy Spirit revealed—that's between them and the Lord.

I was in the spa the other day. I go to the spa once in a while and pump a little iron. Of course, real little, you know. At my age, it isn't body building. It's care and maintenance. And I was in the spa, in the steam room one time, with a fellow, talking about Christ, witnessing to him. Finally he said, "Well, How do I know what to believe?. The Catholics say they're right, and the Baptists say they're right, and this Methodist quotes Scripture, and the Charismatics showed me that so-and-so says this. How do I know which one is right?" I said, "How old are you?" He said, "I'm 22." I said, "You got a college education?" He said, "Yes." I said, "You have a college education." "That's right." I said, "You mean to tell me you're 22 years old and don't know when a man is perverting the Scripture or not?" I said, "You ought to be ashamed of yourself."

"Are you an American with an eighth-grade education? You mean to tell me you can't tell when a man is lying to you, from the pulpit, from the Scripture, and you can't tell? You ought to go soak your head in a bucket three times and pull it out twice. You say, how do you know whether they're teaching the right things or not? You've got the commandment in 1 Thessalonians: 'Prove all things.' Well, I could tell in a half minute if he was misusing the Scripture. You say, 'How?' Open the Scripture and check him out. What do you mean, you can't tell who's right? You ought to be ashamed of yourself.

"If you can read and write, you can buy you a Bible to open it up and see if he is telling you the truth. Maybe he says you ought to pray to blessed Mary, blessed John the Baptist, blessed Joe, that kind of stuff. You ought to be able to turn right to it. There is one mediator between God and man, the man Christ Jesus. There is no problem. Check him out. Check him out. Check him out. If tradition says one thing, and the Bible says another, you should know where they conflict. And you should know where they're correct. sometimes Tradition will line up with the book, sometimes it won't line up with the book. You say I don't know. Hey, Sonny, buy you a book and read it. Can you read? You better get one and read it while you can."

I took my convert course under Father Sullivan, of St. Michael's Church in Pensacola, Florida, who was a Ph.D. from Loyola University. We had quite a time of it. Now, after a while, I finally left and went my way and he went his. And later on, he asked me, "Why did you leave?" I said, "Because I got to the place where I could either believe what the book said or what tradition said." He said, "Yes, but they agree." I said, "I'll show you ten places where they don't." When I showed him the ten places, he said, "Well, where the two conflict, you need the Church. You need an infallible interpreter, an authentic interpreter to show you what it means." I said to myself, "Hey babe, if this is one authority, the Word, and that's the other authority, tradition, and I've got to have a third authority to tell which one's right, I know who the final authority is: it's the third one."

MODERATOR: What we're going to do now is open this thing up for questions. Now, the first thing I'd like to do is ask you to try to make your questions relevant to the subject that has been discussed this morning. The subject has been the inspiration of Scripture. Let's try to gear our questions to that direction. Again, I remind you, your position is to ask a question.

SPEAKER: Mr. Keating, I'm a pastor at a Baptist church. Why are so many Catholics becoming Fundamentalists? What is your feeling on that? Is it the Bible or what?

KEATING: In the last few decades, tens of thousands of Catholics have left the Church and have joined Fundamentalist congregations. That statistic is what prompted me to establish Catholic Answers. This problem—and a Catholic would view it as a problem—is particularly acute among Hispanics in America. As many as one out of six now are Fundamentalists, whereas a few decades years ago you could not find any, almost. To what is this to be attributed? Some Catholics might think the attraction to Fundamentalism is not a matter of theology but of pathology, that a person who leaves the Church for Fundamentalism does so because he's lonely, or he got the brush-off from a priest, or people from the Fundamentalist church came over and shook his hand and patted him on the back. That's a misunderstanding.

I know people who became Fundamentalists, having been Catholics, and who have come back. Some are here tonight. Universally, they say that the first attraction to Fundamentalism was the sincerity, the charity, and, very often the excellent speaking ability of the pastor. Those make a difference, but those are quasi-emotional things. That is not why they became or stayed Fundamentalist. They became and stayed Fundamentalist for doctrinal reasons. Those are the same reasons they cite when they explain why they came back to the Catholic Church.

I have to say that in the last several decades catechesis, instruction in the faith, has been lousy within the Catholic Church. Many people who find a real love for Jesus within the Fundamentalist churches go on to study further. As they continue their journey, they come back to the Catholic Church. Thus the fault is largely among Catholics. For decades, we didn't pay much attention. We figured things would just go on. Now we are paying the piper.

MODERATOR: Is there someone who has a question to direct to Dr. Ruckman? All right, yes sir. Stand up and state it clearly.

SPEAKER: How do we know that we have, in the New Testaments, all the canonical books, that there aren't any extras, there aren't any missing?

RUCKMAN: My answer to that is two-fold. The first answer to that is this: if you are going to trust the Catholic Church at the Council of Carthage, that tells you that the 27 books constitute the New Testament canon, you are going to make a bad mistake because they misled you on the 39 in the Old. If that's the only thing for believing the 27 were inspired in the New Testament, I would say, surely there must have been only 20. Because they just told me there were 46 in the inspired Old Testament books and there wasn't, there were 39. A church that messed up the Old Testament cannot be trusted with the New Testament.

Well, the answer to your question is this, which is very difficult for people to get a hold of. In the New Testament, there is no priest class that needs to determine anything. In the Old Testament, the Levites are in charge of the Scriptures. Therefore, a priesthood, a select chosen priesthood tribe, was in charge of determining what was canonical and what was not. In the New Testament, according to the principal apostle, Simon Peter, all Christians make up a holy priesthood. Therefore, it is left up to the body of believers to determine what books are canonical and which ones aren't. It is not left up to a priest class of scribes meeting in a council to tell you anything. It's left up to the body of believers.

MODERATOR: All right, someone has a question for Mr. Keating. Yes, sir.

SPEAKER: Mr. Keating, I don't know if you have access to a Bible or not. But if you do, I'd like, if you would, please, to interpret one word of Scripture. In 1 Timothy 2:5, the Bible says, "For there is one God and one mediator, between God and men, the man Christ Jesus." Can you explain to us the word "mediator" and the fact that the Bible says there is only one?

KEATING: The word "mediator" means a go-between, but I presume you want a fuller explication than that.

SPEAKER: Yes, sir.

KEATING: The standard objection to the Catholic position on, for example, the veneration of saints is that the Bible says there is one mediator, which is Christ. Quite true, and the Catholic Church acknowledges that. The Catholic Church also says that Christ was free to arrange his mediation in any way he might choose. Now one way is that he told us to pray for one another. I'm sure everyone here at some time, probably daily, prays for the spiritual or physical health of family members and others. What do we do when we do that? We are acting as mediators. When I ask God to protect you, to make you healthy, I am being a mediator. That's what it means.

The Catholic position is that Christ is perfectly at liberty to allow the saints in heaven also to act as mediators. There is no contradiction here. Just as Christ told us to pray for one another here below, we can pray for one another in the hereafter. So there's no contradiction between the two, because the mediation of the saints, any prayer a saint might give, on your behalf is only efficacious because of Christ.

MODERATOR: Mr. Keating was gracious to answer that question. I don't know that he was obligated to because the question at hand is inspiration. Now, we can broaden this thing if these gentlemen are agreeable. But what we have been discussing is inspiration of Scripture. I think it would behoove us well to at least try to conclude any questions that are directed to that subject. I believe there are several that still want to address the subject of inspiration, based on what they've heard. So, if possible, let's try to confine our remarks or questions to that.

SPEAKER: Dr. Ruckman, the question I have, as it regards to the Bible, and we talked about the Bible being the one source of information we can go to, knowing Christ. Before the printing press, all the thousands and millions of souls that were before us, from the time of Christ, up until the fifteenth century—were those people saved through the teaching Church or through the Bible?

RUCKMAN: The idea is until this book came out, how did the people get the truth? How did they get the teaching for four hundred years when there wasn't any New Testament written at all? The answer to your question is found in Romans 2. In Romans 2 you are told that a man is judged by his conscience until his conscience leads him to Christ. After that, he is judged for rejecting or accepting Christ, whether there was any church present or any Scripture present or not. Romans 2:12: "For as many as have sinned without law"—don't have any Bible, don't have any Ten Commandments—"shalt perish without law." They're lost.

The answer to that question is, when Scripture is not available for a fellow, God deals with that fellow and his conscience and will judge that fellow according to his conscience. The prime example is in the Old Testament, where in a dream the Lord says to Abimelech, "You're a dead man. The woman you've got is another man's wife." Right away that bird starts stumbling all over himself and says, "I haven't done a thing wrong." Why does that fellow start stumbling all over himself, if he didn't know "thou shalt not commit adultery"? When God said, "You're a dead man, you've got another fellows wife," you start arguing with God about being innocent. Abimelech didn't know the commandment, he didn't have an Old Testament. So the answer to that is the heathen, without light, are judged by their conscience until they have a chance to receive Christ. After that they are judged for receiving or rejecting Christ. I'm sorry, that goes fast.

SPEAKER: I wish Mr. Keating would comment on a book proving archeologically that the bones of St. Peter were found beneath the Vatican. If you could comment on this book.

KEATING: The book you're referring to is John Evangelist Walsh's *The Bones of St. Peter*. It's a popular account rather than a technical archeological account. It examines the archeological and historical evidence for Peter being in Rome and his bones being found in the necropolis, which is the "city of the dead" underneath St. Peter's Basilica.

What was discovered, in archeological excavations beginning mainly in the 1940s, was that there is indeed a first-century graveyard directly beneath the high altar of St. Peter's Basilica. There are inscriptions on the walls of various tombs saying, "Peter is here" or "Peter is nearby." There was discovered a little tomb in the shape of a niche, identifying itself as the place where Peter was buried. This corresponded to various writings from the early centuries which had said the same thing. The tradition had always been that the first church on that site—not the present Church, of course—the first cathedral there had been built right above Peter's tomb. It turns out, archaeologically, that's a fact.

You have some professional anti-Catholics, such as Loraine Boettner, author of *Roman Catholicism*, which is the main handbook for anti-Catholics, who says there is not one shred of historical evidence that Peter was ever in Rome. Boettner says there's no archeological evidence, but there is a wealth of archeological evidence. We have more evidence to that effect than we have for the location of many other Roman and Greek personages and sites. Archaeologically, there is no doubt that Peter was buried there.

MODERATOR: We are not going to deal with any questions for a while. So we go back to our ten-minute, alternating schedule. Mr. Keating will be first.

KEATING: What I'd like to do, at this point, is discuss Peter and the papacy and papal infallibility. First, Peter's status. We know, from the New Testament, that he had a primacy among the apostles. He always heads the list when they're named. Sometimes, it's just Peter and his companions. He's always in on the most dramatic scenes. He was the first to preach at Pentecost, work the first healing, had the revelation that baptism was for the Gentiles also. Something very special is that, when Christ first saw him, he gave Simon a new name. Most of us don't realize that he gave Simon a non-name. Up to that time, "Peter" was not actually a name. People didn't have the name of

Peter. Christ came up to him and said, "Simon, you are now going to be known as Peter." Whenever we have a name change in the Bible, there is a change in status of the person whose name is changed. Abram was changed to Abraham and Jacob to Israel. You know of others. Every time that happens, it indicates that person's status has been changed in some way. Now, consider where Peter's name change came. Caesarea Philippi, which no longer exists. Today there's a small Arab town of Banias.

One of the headwaters of the Jordan is there. The interesting thing, geologically, is that there's a gigantic wall of rock, 200 feet high, and 500 feet long. Out of it, at the time, came the waters of the Jordan, although it's no longer coming out there. Here it was that Christ said to Simon, "Thou art Peter, and upon this rock I will build my church." He gave him authority when he said, "Whatever you bind on Earth will be bound in heaven. Whatever you loose on Earth will be loosed in heaven." Later the other apostles were given a similar authority, but here Peter is given it in a special way.

I had mentioned, a moment ago, his non-name. If I came up to you and said, "Your name is Sally, or Jack, but hereafter you will be known as Asparagus," you would ask me, "What does that mean? What's the purpose of renaming me?" Why name Simon the Rock? It must signify something. In the Old Testament, only God was called a rock. Here Peter, in some way, is having a participation in God's authority, by Christ's naming him a rock. This isn't to say he's a rock to the exclusion of Christ. Obviously, it must be some secondary foundation that he is being made. Christ also said to him, "I will give to thee—singular—the keys to the kingdom of heaven." Keys, in ancient times, were hallmarks of authority. A walled city would have one gate, opened by one lock, with one key. Peter was given authority over the Kingdom of heaven, which meant the Church here on Earth.

Much mention is made of the Greek, in Matthew 16:18: "Thou art *petros* and upon this *petra* I will build my church." The argument is made, "Well, *petros* and *petra* are different words. *Petra* means a large rock. *Petros* is a stone or a pebble," something, by comparison, insecure. So the argument is *petros*—Peter—cannot be the rock. The rock must be something else, either Christ himself or Peter's affirmation, which appeared in a previous verse. But this obscures something. Christ was not speaking in Greek. The common language of Palestine was Aramaic, and the word in Aramaic is *kepha.*

If we were to put that word into our English sentence, it would read, "Thou art *kepha,* and upon this *kepha* I will build my church." Nobody could mistake that play on words. When Matthew's Gospel was translated into Greek, the word *petra* could be used for *kepha,* large rock, but it could not be used for the name of Simon. In Greek nouns have endings according to gender. *Petra* is feminine. You cannot use it as a man's name. But if you give it a masculine ending, you have *petros,* a pre-existing word that means stone. You lose something of the play on words.

RUCKMAN: The term *pope* doesn't occur anywhere in history until 366 A.D. That's in the *Catholic Encyclopedia,* volume 12, page 270. The idea of the primacy of Peter is an interesting thing, but let's, for fun, turn to the passage we were discussing, Matthew 16. Nothing like a Bible to clear up a Bible conference. The gentleman removed two verses from the entire context. He didn't give you the context. The context is very interesting. Now we Bible-believing Protestants say the rock is Jesus Christ. He says it's Simon Peter. Obviously we have two different rocks. Let's see what this rock here is. Verse 22, which he did not read: "Then Peter took him and began to rebuke him saying, be it far from me Lord, they should not be unto thee; but he turned and said to Peter, Get thee behind Me," who?

PEOPLE: Satan.

RUCKMAN: Who?

PEOPLE: Satan.

RUCKMAN: Oh, you're interpreting. No, you're not interpreting, you're reading. You know who Jesus said that to? He said that to Simon Peter. He called him the Devil. If your church is built on Simon Peter, you have a rough foundation. Now take your Bible and turn to 1 Corinthians 10 and let's look at the difference here. This is Paul writing: "And yet all drank that spiritual drink, and they drank of that spiritual rock that followed them. And that rock was Christ."

You know what "Simon" means? Shifting sand. Look it up in a Greek dictionary. Simon's first name is shifting sand, his new name had to do with the rock, but not the rock our church is built upon. The rock his church is built upon. He and I can both come to one agreement. We can both come to the agreement we have different rocks. We have two different kinds of wine we drink of, as well as two rocks. This gentleman drinks fermented liquor at the Mass. We drink grape juice, at the Lord's Supper. So our vine's not the same, and our rock's not the same. Aren't we going to have a time getting together ecumenically?

If Peter was at Rome, here's the question. In Romans 16, the last chapter in the book of Romans, Paul gives sends his greetings to 25 Christians at Rome and doesn't mention the pastor. If Peter is the Vicar of Christ and head of the first Church at Rome, why is it when Paul, the apostle of the Gentiles, writes to the Romans, he won't mention the head of the Church? I never saw such a breach of etiquette in all my life. What an unethical thing to do, to greet all these fellows in Rome and then forget to say hello to the bishop of Rome.

KEATING: Presumably Peter was out of town at the time, and Paul knew it. We know Peter went to the Council of Jerusalem around A.D. 49, for example. There is no reason to think he was always in Rome, and the Catholic Church has never claimed that. To note his name not being not mentioned doesn't prove much. Another thing that doesn't prove much is the fact that the word "pope" was not used until 366 or whatever year. Does that prove that the papacy does not exist? If so, then you would have to say the Trinity does not exist because that word was not used before 181.

The word "pope" comes from the Greek *papa*, which means father. It's merely an honorific. The office can exist without that particular title. In fact Dr. Ruckman didn't bring this up but he could have—at first it wasn't even restricted to the bishop of Rome. All the major bishops, for a few centuries, were using the title. The Coptic patriarch, in Alexandria, is still known as the pope. He's not a Catholic, but he is known as the pope today. So the use of a word, whether "pope" or "Trinity" or "Transubstantiation"—the use of the technical term doesn't prove anything as to when the doctrine was first believed.

I want to start talking about papal infallibility, and I want to begin with what it is not. It is not what many Fundamentalists believe. It is not impeccability. The Catholic position is not that a pope cannot sin. So, please, in your questions do not say, "But didn't pope so-and-so commit this sin?" He may very well have, but that has nothing to do with the question of infallibility. Infallibility means the inability, when teaching officially, to teach an error in faith or in morals. It's limited to faith and morals. If the pope tries to predict the World Series winner, his guess is no better than yours or mine. If he teaches officially that Christ rose from the dead and that the Resurrection is not symbolic but historical, he teaches infallibly. His infallible teaching extends to doctrine about faith and morals, and he must be teaching officially, not in private, not over the dinner table to his neighbor.

I mentioned earlier Loraine Boettner's book *Roman Catholicism*. I know quite a few of you have read it. You might remember that passage where he talks about papal infallibility. He quotes Vatican I, in 1870. Boettner says, "Well, the Catholic Church position is that the pope is infallible only when he speaks *ex cathedra*, Latin for 'from the throne,' 'from the chair.' Therefore, he's infallible only when he is seated in Peter's chair. We know that what is venerated as Peter's chair, at St. Peter's Basilica, is probably only from the ninth century and of French origin. Therefore, even if the pope theoretically has the power, he could issue no infallible opinion because he can't sit in the real chair that Peter used."

That's not what *ex cathedra* means. When a judge issues a judgment, we say he rules from the bench. He doesn't have to be sitting on the bench. He can be in the courthouse hallway, and his judgment is still official. When Catholics say that Peter speaks *ex cathedra*, that just means he speaks officially, with the intent that what he's saying is to be held as true. He doesn't often exercise that power, and when he does, it's clear that he is doing it.

"He who listens to you, listens to me," Christ said. "All that you bind on Earth shall be bound in heaven." Infallibility belongs to all the bishops when teaching in union with the pope. This is a doctrine that hasn't changed, and it was repeated by Vatican II. The pope has the ability to teach infallibly by himself. The bishops of the world gathered together in ecumenical council can teach infallibly too, so long as their teaching is ratified by the pope.

"I've prayed for thee that thy faith may not fail." "Feed my sheep." "Thou art Peter." Those are the three main verses on which papal infallibility rests. I'll discuss a little more about it next time.

RUCKMAN: The Trinity turns out to be a biblical doctrine. If the papacy turns out to be a biblical doctrine then we'll accept it. If it doesn't, we'll throw it out. He quoted Eusebius. When a Catholic wants to prove something contrary to Scripture, he goes to the Church Fathers. Those are Ignatius, Polycarp, Tertullian, Justin Martyr, and the like. Martin Luther used to say some of the Church Fathers ought to be called the Church babies. That's our sentiments, exactly.

In regarding the pope speaking infallibly, he doesn't do it often—that's a masterpiece of understatement. He's only done it twice. He made one statement about Mary's Immaculate Conception, being born sinless, and one time about Mary being assumed into heaven, the Assumption of Mary.

In regards to Peter's power, and the loosing in heaven and Earth that he's quoted, I don't think you realize what that means. So I'll read you from *A Catechism for Adults*. "Question: when did Jesus promise to make Peter the pope? Answer: several months before he died. Question: when did Jesus actually make Peter the first pope? Answer: shortly before he ascended into heaven. Question: who will go to hell? Answer: only those who die with mortal sin on their souls. Question: who has power to forgive sin today? Answer: all bishops and priests of the Catholic Church can forgive sin."

Will you pardon a personal interjection? Bologna. I'm not worried about some Catholic priest or bishop forgiving my sins. Let him go play with his little push cart. Nothing to me one way or another. I received forgiveness for my sins the fourteenth of March, 1949, at 10:30 in the morning in downtown Pensacola, Florida.

KEATING: Some small corrections first. Tertullian was not a Church Father. He was a Montanist heretic at this death. He's never been considered, by Catholics, to be a Father of the Church. Fathers of the Church were those whose writings were not heretical. Second, in the last century-and-a-half, there have been more than two times when the pope has exercised what's known as his extraordinary magisterium to define a doctrine. But it happens fairly commonly, in every canonization. The Church is saying that this person's life is worthy of emulation and he is now in heaven. The Church has to be able to say that accurately. You can't very well set up for emulation somebody who's now in hell. In ages gone by there were other instances of the papacy teaching infallibly.

Let me turn to the forgiveness of sins. Christ himself forgave sins. It's mentioned several times in the Gospels. He did this as man, in and through his human nature. He said, "This is done to convince you that the Son of Man has the authority to forgive while he is on Earth." Now since he wouldn't always be on Earth, he gave this power to the apostles. And since they also would not always be on Earth, the power must be communicable. It's passed down through the bishops. We read that Christ breathed on the apostles and said to them, "Receive the Holy Spirit. When you forgive men's sins, they are forgiven. When you hold them bound, they are held bound." This is one of only two times in the whole Bible that God breathed on man, the other being Genesis 2:7, when he made man a living soul. Something key is going on here. He told the apostles to go out and gave them authority. "As the Father sent me, so am I sending you." What he did, they were to do.

The power to forgive sins definitely was not from themselves. "This, as always, is God's doing. It is he who, through Christ, has reconciled us to himself, and allowed us to minister his reconciliation to others." People try to say, look, when it said, "Whose sins you shall forgive, they are forgiven, whose sins you shall retain, they are retained"—that just meant the power to declare sins already forgiven. That doesn't wash. It doesn't say anything about telling people their sins already are forgiven if they accept Jesus. It doesn't say that. You have to do violence to the text to get that out of it. It's very clearly giving the apostles the power to forgive.

If this power didn't exist in New Testament times, one thing we should expect to see is a big uproar in early Christian literature. We should be able to find records of protest about this usurpation. There are none. We do not find any Christian writers of the early centuries saying, "Christ did not give the apostles the power to forgive sins."

We have records from the early centuries that say that a Christian is to confess his sins to a priest. Origen? Not a Father of the Church, but an early Christian writer testifying to this. Cyprian in the year 251, Methodius a century later. The power to forgive sins, or to hold them bound, necessarily implies that the priest has to be told the sins. He can't forgive what he doesn't know about. Therefore, you have, ultimately, auricular confession. "Auricular" means "to the ear." In the early Church, confession was public. You confessed your sins in front of the whole congregation. In a few centuries that practice was discontinued. There were obvious psychological difficulties with that. Many people would not confess at all or would stay away from church.

In the Catholic doctrine of the priestly power to forgive, there is no contradiction with the notion of Christ being the one mediator. Every Catholic theology manual acknowledges that. It points out that there's no contradiction because Christ could arrange things however he wished. He didn't have to become man for us—he could have just willed our salvation— but he became incarnated and took flesh. He wasn't forced to do it that way. He could have just decided that we just pray to him and that's it, and our sins are forgiven.

The Catholic position is that sins indeed can be forgiven if you pray and are sincerely contrite, sincerely repentant. But the reason confession was instituted is that we can't usually tell whether we're sufficiently contrite or are fooling ourselves. It's a common human failing. We're all subject to it. We tend to have favorite sins that we do over and over, and we can fool ourselves into thinking that we're sorry for them when we're not really.

It's often said that confession makes it too easy for Catholics. You sin on

Friday, you go to confession on Saturday, and you're ready to sin the next week. Actually it's easier from the Fundamentalist's point of view because all you have to do is go to your bedroom and pray. You don't have to tell a priest. And then you too go out and sin again. So if that's an argument of convenience against the Catholic position, there is more of an argument against the Fundamentalist position.

When Christ said that the apostles had been given the power to forgive, he wasn't saying they had the power to declare somebody forgiven. It's not what those words are saying. He said, "Whose sins you shall forgive, they are forgiven." I don't see what could be any plainer than that. All the Christians understood that's what he meant. The notion that there was no priestly power to forgive came about fifteen centuries later.

MODERATOR: Let's take questions again.

SPEAKER: This is directed toward Mr. Keating. If you say that the Bible is the inspired word of God, where is your Bible? Why is it that I can walk into the Catholic church, in my hometown today, and not find one Bible but instead a missalette?

KEATING: People have different ways of speaking, different styles. If you were to see my notes, you'd see that everything I've quoted from the Bible has a reference. I don't believe in giving chapter and verse, because it's a waste of time. I presume that most of you know the verses. Second, I didn't bring my Bible because I don't like to flip through pages and read from it to the audience. I prefer to use notes. I don't think I need to use the Bible as a prop.

Regarding your other question, the missalette gives the words that are used in the Mass. If you look through the missalette, you'll find it's mainly made up of selections from the Bible. It has the Bible readings that are pertinent to the Mass of the day.

SPEAKER: What about "Call no man your father"?

KEATING: Paul wrote telling some people that they were his children in faith, that he was their father. When we call a priest "Father," what we mean, and the reason he's given the title, is because at baptism he regenerates us. The notion of fatherhood deals with generation, the giving of life. The priest, by administering baptism, effects a spiritual regeneration. We believe that baptism confers grace. It actually does something to us. If you are going to use a terribly literalistic sense of "Call no man your father," then you are going to have a problem regarding your mother's husband.

SPEAKER: You made a statement, "Why should the Bible be taken as a rule of faith"? Do you believe there is more than one rule of faith?

KEATING: The Catholic position is that the Bible alone was never meant to be the rule of faith, that the notion of sola scriptura is improper. The true rule of faith is Scripture plus Tradition. By Tradition, I don't mean customs, I don't mean habits, I don't mean styles of dress. It's unfortunate that we have one word having several meanings. That's not what Tradition means. Tradition, in the Catholic theological sense, is the continuation of the oral teachings of the apostles through the living Church, the living magisterium, which means teaching authority. Fundamentalists would not acknowledge the existence of that teaching authority, since Fundamentalists do not acknowledge a visible, hierarchical Church. When I was asking whether we should take the Bible as the rule of faith, I was referring, of course, to the Fundamentalist position, which is that the Bible is the sole rule of faith.

MODERATOR: Does someone have a question for Dr. Ruckman? Yes sir, in the checkered shirt.

SPEAKER: Dr. Ruckman, before I got saved, I was raised Catholic. When I went through parochial school, in catechism classes they taught us the Ten Commandments. After I got saved, I discovered that the Ten Commandments that I was taught were not the same Ten Commandments that the Bible speaks about. Namely, the second Commandment is omitted in the catechism, and the Tenth Commandment is split up into two commandments. Could you comment on that, please?

RUCKMAN: The official teaching of the Roman Catholic Church is there is no commandment forbidding you to have graven images. There is no second commandment in the Catholic Church. You say, how did they get ten? They take the last one and bust it down into two. Nice piece of work, baby. Ninth commandment, "Thou shall not covet thy neighbor's wife." Tenth commandment, "Thou shall not covet thy neighbor's goods." So you make two out of one and that way you get rid of the commandment to prevent you from having graven images. That means somebody wants you to have graven images. If they don't, what did they take it out for?

MODERATOR: We will again begin a debate format.

KEATING: I ought to say something, I suppose, about the Mass, because those of you who never have been Catholics may not know what happens at the Mass. I debated, a while back, another Fundamentalist minister, and someone from the audience said, "You people never hear anything about the Bible at Mass." I explained to her that the Mass is divided into two parts. The first part is called the Liturgy of the Word, where we have readings from the Bible. At Sunday Mass there are four of them. The first is a reading from the Old Testament. Then, one of the psalms is read, often sung. Then comes a reading from the New Testament, other than Gospels. The fourth selection comes from one of the Gospels.

Each day during the year, a different set of readings is given. There is a three-year cycle of readings, so that, in a Catholic church, if you were to attend daily Mass, in three years you would hear read out to you virtually all of the New Testament and a very large portion of the Old.

I submit to you that if you belong to a Fundamentalist congregation, you don't hear nearly that much of the Bible read out. Different Fundamentalist congregations are different. Some will concentrate on the rapture or eternal security or some other doctrine and will go over and over such points but leave out large parts of the Bible otherwise—not that you're discouraged from reading it, but those other parts are not part of the service. I would dispute anybody who says that the average Catholic hears less of the Bible than the average Fundamentalist. If he goes to daily Mass, he hears quite more.

Now let me go on to another topic to which Dr. Ruckman alluded, namely salvation and our assurance. Several people, during the break, asked me about it. The Fundamentalist notion is that, after accepting Christ, one's salvation is guaranteed. No sin can undo it. It doesn't matter what sin you may commit later, you will not be condemned to hell for it. The Catholic idea, obviously, is different. The Catholic idea is that your salvation, which is to say, getting into heaven, is dependent upon the state of your soul when you die.

If we were to be transported now to the Moon, we would die. We are not equipped to live on the Moon, where there is no air. We need special equipment to live there—equipment that is above out nature: supernatural, so to speak. Same for heaven. We are not naturally equipped for heaven. We must be filled with supernatural grace. The Catholic Church says that only a soul in the state of grace is able to enjoy heaven. If you are not grace filled—if you have a dead soul, from which grace is absent—you go to hell. This means that it's possible for anyone to be saved, possible for anyone to go to hell. It does depend how you die, what the state of your soul is at death.

A Fundamentalist will say, not so. The soul remains depraved. Your sinful condition stays but is covered, as by a cloak. The righteousness of Christ is imputed to you. Your soul, though, does not become itself holy. The Catholic position is that through grace your soul becomes holy and good.

I was talking some months ago with Bart Brewer of Mission To Catholics. You may know of Bart, an ex-priest who tries to convert people to Fundamentalism. He was pointing out priestly sins. I said to him, Bart, what about pastor so-and-so, who had been an institutional supporter of your group? He was arrested for child molestation, a serious sin. Are you telling me that, under your own theory, this man is just as saved as the fellow in your congregation who "gets saved" and then immediately dies, never having a chance to sin? Bart had to say, sure, that's our position, which, I think, is a repugnant position because it leads to antinomianism, which is lawlessness.

If there is nothing you can do after being saved that will affect your salvation, why not have fun, here below, while the having's good? There is nothing you can do, no matter how perverse, that could condemn you, on Bart's theory. That's not the Catholic theory. The Catholic theory is that you must remain grace-filled.

When I moved to my present home, a few days later, the minister of the Fundamentalist church across the way came to the door. I invited him in. We had a nice talk. The first question he asked is: "Do you have an assurance of salvation?" I said "No, because it's not biblical." He had never heard anybody say that before. We had a nice discussion.

RUCKMAN: Now, what happens when a Christian sins? Talk about preachers in jail for child molestation. Yes, we had a case of a Catholic priest, down in Louisiana, last year. All over the newspapers for about four or five months. Parents wanted to sue him, and the Catholic Church tried to buy the parents off so it wouldn't become a public scandal. Common news in the *Picayune*. You don't believe it, go read it. I'll show you what happens when a Christian sins. I'll show you what happens when you become a child of God and don't live right.

1 Corinthians 11:30: "For this cause many are weak and sickly among you"—sick Christians—"and many sleep"—dead Christians. Verse 31: "For if we would judge ourselves, we should not be judged." But when we are judged, we don't go to hell. When we're judged, we're chastened of the Lord. You know what God does with the sin, in the Christian? He whips him. He takes out the belt. Whom the Lord loveth, he chasteneth. If you endure chastening, God deals with you as a son, for what son is he whom the Father chasteneth not?

This ridiculous idea that you have to be born again and again and again is nonsense. You are born again or you're not born again. I've got three sons, Peter, Michael, and David. They are born of my seed. You know when they cease to be my sons? Never. You know why? They can't be born again, out of their mother's womb. Those boys will be Ruckmans when they're dead,

Ruckmans on their tombstone. If they change their names, they'd still be Ruckmans, because they're born of my seed. How many of you have been born of incorruptible seed, by the word of God? Let me see your hands. All right then, be careful how you live. But you ain't going to change your family, no matter what happens. Even if God has to kill you.

KEATING: Let's look at a few verses that he forgot to mention, such as 1 Corinthians 9:27: "I buffet my own body and make it my slave, for I, who have preached to others, may myself be rejected as worthless." I use the Ronald Knox translation; yours is similar. I can talk later about the question of the King James, if you wish, but I prefer an accurate translation. But the essence of the passage under either is the same.

What Paul is saying here is that he might be lost. "You must work to earn your salvation in anxious fear." Now what did he mean by that? That's not the language of self-confident assurance. He's had the Damascus road experience already, so if anyone was ever born again, surely it was he. "All of us have a scrutiny to undergo before Christ's judgment seat"—this is 2 Corinthians 5:10—"for each to reap what his mortal life has earned, good or ill, according to his deeds." And Romans 2:6: "God will award to every man what his acts have deserved." Under the Fundamentalist notion, that doesn't have anything to do with salvation.

Luther, as you well know, or as you should know, mistranslated when he said that "salvation is by faith alone." He took the Latin Vulgate and added the word "alone" in the margin. The word "alone" doesn't appear in the original Greek, but he had to put that in because the text, he realized, didn't otherwise support the salvation-by-faith-alone theory. At Romans 5:2, Paul says, "We are confident in the hope of attaining glory as the sons of God." Now saints in heaven do not exercise the virtues of hope or faith. A saint has no need of hope because he already is in heaven. A saint in heaven has no need of faith because he sees God. He has charity in perfect abundance. Of the three theological virtues, that's the only one you find in heaven.

"Our salvation is founded on the hope of something"—Romans 8:28— "Hope would not be hope at all if its object were in view." How could a man still hope for something he sees? How could a man still hope for something he has absolute assurance of? That's contradictory. There is no need to hope for something you have absolute assurance of getting. If salvation were as assured as the Fundamentalist might think, then this hope that Paul talks about is meaningless. There would be no purpose to it. When Paul says that he might be lost, that doesn't fit in either. You can have a moral certainty of salvation, but you can't really have absolute assurance, and the reason you can't is because it doesn't mesh with other verses in the New Testament.

MODERATOR: We are going to open it up for questions again. This gentleman down here.

SPEAKER: My question is for both of the men. What is their definition of Fundamentalism?

KEATING: This may be something I should have brought up initially. Many people use the term "Fundamentalist" in a purely pejorative sense. I do not. The trouble with terminology is that often we can't find a precise enough word. I think it's easy enough, if I say "Catholic," that you understand what I'm talking about. What word am I to choose, otherwise? Some people would say well, "I prefer Evangelical." Well that's a wide word, and it goes from liberal Protestantism and overlaps Fundamentalism. Most of those are not people I'm talking about. Others say, "Well we're just Bible Christians." Again, that's imprecise; besides, I believe that Catholics are as much Bible Christians as you are. So, that's not a precise term.

Unfortunately, there really isn't a perfectly precise term. I use "Fundamentalism" in a narrow sense but not in a pejorative sense. If you are familiar with the books called *The Fundamentals* written about 1915-1919. The principles enunciated in those, that kind of faith is what I'm talking about when I mean Fundamentalism. Some people that I would call Fundamentalists don't like to use the term. Others welcome it. There is considerable variety. I just don't know of any other word that is more accurate.

MODERATOR: All right. The gentleman in the green.

SPEAKER: My question is to Mr. Keating. In Psalms, God said that he holds his word above his name. Also in Psalms he says his word will endure forever. I can't quote the verse verbatim right now. If that's so, how come you made that statement that you believe the Bible is not a rule of faith?

KEATING: What I believe is not that the Bible is not a rule of faith but that it is not the sole rule of faith. The Catholic position is that the Bible plus Tradition make the rule of faith. We don't throw the Bible out and replace it with something else. There are two founts, as Vatican II put it, two sources of faith, which must be taken together.

SPEAKER: Dr. Ruckman, could you give us some Bible verses on tradition as opposed to Scripture?

RUCKMAN: Yes, there are many of them. I'll show you the main one. So far you've been given tradition as an equal authority with the Word of God, without any regard for the particular nature of that tradition. And the nature of that tradition has been citations from the Church Fathers. Mark 7 was written before there were any Church Fathers.

Mark 7:5: "Then the Pharisees and scribes asked him why walk not thy disciples according to the tradition of the elders?" Verse 6: "Well did Isaiah prophesy of you hypocrites. It is written, this people honors me with their lips but their heart is far from me. How be it in vain do they worship me, teaching for doctrine the commandments of men?" Verse 9: "And he said of them full well you reject the commandment of God, that you may keep your own tradition."

MODERATOR: All right. I think we'll just take one or two more. Gentleman back there on the aisle.

SPEAKER: Being a non-Fundamentalist and a non-Catholic, I'd like to ask both of you a question. The question is on the assurance of salvation. Does the Baptist believe that one who is a practicing Catholic and a member of the Catholic Church will have any problem on judgment day, and vise-versa for the Catholic?

MODERATOR: All right. As I understand it, the question is do both groups believe that the other one will have problems on judgment day. Mr. Keating, you're first.

KEATING: I think the real question is, to narrow it down, do they have any hope on judgment day? The Catholic position is that non-Catholics can be saved. The Bible says that we must be born again through water and the Holy Spirit. The Catholic Church understands that to be baptism and that there are really three forms of baptism. One is sacramental, water baptism. Another is the martyr's death, baptism of blood. The third is baptism of desire, which is not a sacrament; it's where a person, in what the Church calls invincible ignorance, tries to do good and lives a life according to the lights given him.

So the Catholic position is that a Jew, a Muslim, a non-believer, or a Protestant can be saved but not necessarily that they would have the same likelihood as a Catholic, all things else being equal. The Catholic has the advantage of recourse to the sacraments, which most non-Catholics don't, and to the full teaching of Christian truth. So there are great advantages to being a Catholic. But, is it possible that a non-Catholic can be saved? Yes.

MODERATOR: All right. Dr. Ruckman?

RUCKMAN: My answer, very quickly, is I believe many Catholics are saved, in spite of what some of the brethren think or how anti-Catholic you may think I am. I've talked to hundreds of Catholics in America who I think were truly born-again Christians and children of God, in spite of their Church's teachings. I say that because I'm about to quote the Church's teachings from the most important council they ever had. What I'm quoting you is not what Mr. Keating just said. What I'm quoting you is from the largest official, most important council the Catholic Church ever held. The Council of Trent takes the first place, not only because of its restatement of Catholic doctrine but because of its extraordinary influence both within and without the Church.

No Baptist believes that Roman Catholic water baptism saves anybody. There isn't a Baptist in this church that believes that. So according to the Catholics, he's an anathema. Not according to Mr. Keating but according to the Council of Trent. "If anyone say that baptism is optional, that it is not necessary for salvation, let him be anathema." Whoever heard of a Baptist saying if you don't believe what I believe, you're anathema? Whoever heard of such intolerant bigoted, narrow-minded, prejudiced dogmatism?

I didn't write that. That's official Catholic literature, of the most important council they ever held. According to that, there isn't a saved Baptist in this room. I would say this: any Catholic can be saved by simply believing in the Lord Jesus Christ and receiving him as his Savior. I'll go even further than that. Show you how much grace I've got. A great deal more grace than some of you narrow-minded bigots.

I might even suggest that perhaps Mr. Keating is saved. I don't know already what he is trusting. He may not have told the whole truth about exactly what he's trusting, but I'm sure he believes Christ is Virgin born. I'm sure he believes he died on the Cross. I'm sure he believed he rose from the dead. I'm sure Mr. Keating, in his heart, wants to please the Lord. I don't know whether Mr. Keating has personally received Christ himself, not as a wafer but as a Savior. If he has, he is just as saved as I am. He just isn't enjoying it.

KEATING: I'm going to take a few seconds to reply to that because the impression you have been left with is that anybody who is anathematized is condemned to hell. Is that what you understood it to mean? That's not what it means. In a Catholic ecumenical council, the anathema means you are excommunicated. That is, you are no longer a member of the Catholic Church. You're no longer a Catholic because you don't believe what the Catholic Church believes. Truth in advertising.

The Catholic Church has never condemned people to hell. As a matter of fact, it is not even a doctrine that Judas is in hell. There is no official infallible statement that any particular individual is in hell. When you read something that says you're anathematized, it means you're no longer a member of this club. Don't read into it what isn't there.

Another point is that the council Fathers were addressing Catholics. None of that applies to non-Catholics. You can't be a heretic if you are not a Catholic to begin with. A heretic is a Catholic who understands the truth of the Catholic faith or a doctrine and then rejects it. That's the only way you can be a heretic.

RUCKMAN: I'll give Mr. Keating grounds on this: there are some verses in the New Testament that would seem to teach Christians can lose salvation. Turn back to 1 Corinthians 9 that he quoted you before the break and show how he took the verse clean out of the whole chapter. In the legal practice where he practices law, a text without a context is a pretext, and he took 1 Corinthians 9:27 clean out of the chapter. Notice the chapter had nothing to do with salvation at all. First of all look at verse 5, and notice that Cephas, Simon Peter, was a married pope. Look at 9:5. Simon Peter was married. He had a mother-in-law who was sick in Matthew 8. The entire chapter is talking about a ministry, and there's no discussion in this chapter about an individual being lost at all. He was talking about the salvation of a ministry when he said, "When I have preached to others, I, myself, should be cast away."

Now come to 1 Timothy and watch the same thing again. In 1 Timothy 4:16 notice how even the word "saved" sometimes does not refer to the salvation of a man's soul at all but the salvation of his ministry. "Take ye to thyself and to the doctrine, continue in them, for enduring this, thou shalt save thyself." Look at the context. Verse 12, ministry; verse 13, ministry; verse 14, ministry; verse 15, ministry. He's talking about the salvation of the ministry.

One more time, Romans 8. Mr. Keating went to some degree talking about hope and faith, and again he forgot to show you the context. I'll show you what he was quoting. He was quoting Romans 8:24 and forgot to read to you verse 22 and verse 23, and the context of Roman 8 had nothing to do with you getting to heaven at all. Look at the passage, Romans 8:22. "For we know the whole creation groaneth and travaileth in pain together until now. And not only they but ourselves also, which have the first fruits of the Spirit, even we ourselves groan within ourselves, waiting for the adoption, to wit, the redemption of our"—what?

PEOPLE: Bodies.

RUCKMAN: What?

PEOPLE: Bodies.

RUCKMAN: Again.

PEOPLE: Bodies.

RUCKMAN: Again.

PEOPLE: Bodies.

RUCKMAN: Again.

PEOPLE: Bodies.

RUCKMAN: no salvation of the soul in the passage. No reference of salvation of the soul in all of that passage. It's talking about the salvation of your body at the second advent. He left out the first verse. That made you think you were waiting to see whether or not you're gonna get to heaven.

KEATING: Dr. Ruckman made a reference to Peter being married. A lot of Fundamentalists bring that up to Catholics as though Catholics were to be surprised by it, when, in fact, it's something well-known to Catholics, and Catholics, at least I, respond by saying yes, and did you know even today many priests in the Eastern Rite Catholic Churches are married, and some of the early popes were married? Sort of an immaterial point. This brings to mind a Fundamentalist perception of the origin of Catholicism. I mean the notion that Catholicism is real Christianity but with the addition of non-scriptural or non-Christian pagan influences. There seem to be two basic versions of its history, what I call the pagan convert theory and the Babylonian cult theory.

The pagan convert theory—something Loraine Boettner, for example, pushes, as do many other professional anti-Catholics—says, "Look, here are many Catholic inventions," as they're termed, things that were not mentioned directly in the Bible and were brought up some centuries later. The anti-Catholics' lists always start in the fourth century. They say what really happened is that when Constantine in 313 legalized Christianity—he didn't make it the official religion; that was a lifetime later—when he legalized Christianity, pagans entered the Christian Church in hopes of secular and political preferment. There were so many newcomers that there wasn't time to catechize them properly, so they brought in their customs, and the Catholic Church developed out of the original Christian Church taking on these foreign things.

That particular theory breaks down because of the dating. Everything depends on the legalization of Christianity in 313. You can look at early Christian writers and may disagree with their beliefs, but in the second and third centuries, long before this legalization, they're mentioning prayers for the dead, the veneration of saints, the Eucharist as the real body and blood of Christ—the kinds of things we say are peculiarly Catholic beliefs.

Some Fundamentalists point out that, according to Cardinal John Henry Newman, such things as incense, lamps, candles, votive offerings, and sacerdotal vestments are all of pagan origin. Quite true. Also quite irrelevant. Most of you who are Fundamentalists and who are married I presume were married in a church ceremony. Probably the bride wore white, carried a bouquet, maybe had on a veil. After the vows, rings were exchanged. Are you aware that the exchanging of rings, the wearing of a veil, the wearing of a white dress, the holding of a bouquet are all of pagan origin? They are. Does that mean Fundamentalism came from paganism? Of course not. Similarity does not imply descent.

What I mentioned is the standard anti-Catholic history. There is a more exotic history, the idea that Catholicism arose from Babylonian cult worship. The chief writers for that are two. One was Alexander Hislop who wrote in 1853 *The Two Babylons*. More recently, Ralph Woodrow wrote *Babylon Mystery Religion*. They don't understand the nature of the non-Christian religions of ancient times, and their proofs are laughable. In Woodrow's case, most of his "facts" about what the Babylonian religion was are wrong, even before he gets to the point of comparing it to Catholicism. He doesn't identify what the Babylonians believed or the Egyptians or others.

So the first theory, what I call the pagan convert theory, falls apart because of the dating. You can look back at the Fathers of the Church and other Christian writers that Catholics would not consider Fathers. You can read even those considered heretics by Catholic standards. They all refer to Catholic practices—confession, the Eucharist, the Mass—as existing prior to Constantine. On the other hand, the more exotic theory, of the Babylonian origin—again, there's no basis to that.

What both Catholics and Protestants need to do is to go back and to read a good history. There are good histories by Protestants as well as Catholics. A particularly good history by a Catholic is Philip Hughes' three-volume *History of the Church*. He was a Catholic priest. You would find nothing, I think, objectionable in his explication of the facts, though you perhaps would differ in some interpretations. Don't worry. You won't automatically be converted just by reading a Catholic-written book. I hope that you read such books because you'd find out the history that professional anti-Catholics give about where Catholicism came from is bunk, and you should know it.

RUCKMAN: Now I'm going to close my session here with Romans 4, and I won't have any more to say this afternoon. I'm about through for a while. I'm going to close with Romans 4:5–8, and before I sit down, I'd like to illustrate what a Bible-believing Baptist means when he talks about eternal spirit. Romans 4:5: "But to him that worketh not, that believeth on him that justifies the ungodly, his faith is counted for righteousness even as David also describeth the blessedness of the man unto whom God inputeth righteousness without works, saying blessed are they whose iniquities are forgiven, and whose sins are covered." Hear the verse: "Blessed is the man to whom the Lord will not impute sin." Here's a fellow that's sinned, and God won't charge him with it. "Blessed is the man to whom the Lord will not impute sin." We call that imputation. I'll show you what that means.

Here's a diary, life of Peter S. Ruckman, filled with sins. There are mistakes, godless depravity, every kind of sin. You name it, it's there. Here's the life of Jesus Christ, spotless, perfect, sinless, Holy Son of God. I've come to Christ and taken him as my Savior. God takes this book here, and writes across it, "This is the life of my Son, Jesus Christ," and God imputes my sins to him. Behold the Lamb of God. Christ became sin for us, he who knew no sin, who bore on his body my sins on the cross. He takes my filth and my dirt and with his stripes I'm healed, and my crime is just laid on him. My dirty rotten life is imputed to Jesus Christ. This is the life of Peter S. Ruckman.

I get God's imputed righteousness when I trust Christ. When I trust Christ, God gives me his righteousness. Romans 10:1-10: "Brethren, my heart's desire and prayer for Israel is that they might be saved, for I bear them record that they have a zeal of God, but not according to knowledge, for they being ignorant of God's righteousness and going about to establish their own righteousness have not submitted themselves unto the righteousness of God, for Christ is the end of the law for righteousness for everyone that believeth."

All right. I'm through for today. I enjoyed it. Enjoyed it. Had a good time.

KEATING: Well, since he's through for today, I guess this will have to be my last. I'd enjoy going on for another hour solo, but that hardly would be fair.

I'm going to turn to the subject of the brethren of the Lord and what that means, particularly with reference to whether Mary was perpetually a virgin. That's the Catholic position, of course, that she was a virgin both before and after, even during, Christ's birth. Several verses refer to people called Christ's brethren. Fundamentalists conclude that these people are the actual blood brothers of Christ, brothers german.

The word "brother" had a wide meaning in the Bible. Lot is called Abraham's brother even though he was his nephew. Jacob is called the brother of his Uncle Laban. Sis and Eleazar were the sons of Moholi. Now Sis had sons, and Eleazar had daughters, and we're told that the daughters married their "brethren" who were the sons of Sis, but they really married their cousins. Sometimes the word "brethren" meant kinsman as in 1 Kings 10:13 or just a friend or just an ally as in Amos 1:9. The ambiguous usage was there because neither Aramaic nor Hebrew had a word for cousin in our sense of the word. When the Septuagint translation was made, Hebrew to Greek, the translators used the Greek for brother even though a Greek word existed for cousin. They made a transliteration of those terms rather than a translation.

At the Annunciation, Mary asked the angel, "How can this be since I know not man?" The Catholic Church understands this to imply a vow of life-long virginity. Certainly Mary knew the rudiments of biology. She knew where babies come from. Her comment would have made no sense at all if it was her intention to have several children. She wouldn't have to ask how could that be. It's obvious how it could be, the way everybody else had children. We note that when Christ was found in the Temple, he was called *the* son of Mary, not *a* son. The Greek there implies an only son.

What's more, those who are called the brethren of the Lord are never called Mary's sons. It's a rather odd usage if they were her sons. Something that a lot of us miss is that the brethren gave Jesus advice: leave Galilee, go to Judea, preach there. If Mary had children after Jesus—obviously not before since we know he was the firstborn—then they must have been younger than he. In Oriental societies today, as in the Palestine of ancient times, it is improper for a younger son to give advice to an older, but it would be okay for younger, more distant relatives or friends to do so.

There are two objections, based on one verse, to Mary's perpetual virginity. The verse is Matthew 1:25: "Then he knew her not until she brought forth her firstborn son." First look at "until." 2 Kings 7:23: "Michal the daughter of Saul had no children until the day of her death." This doesn't mean she had children after her death. Here, "until" tells us she never had any children. When the raven went forth from the ark in Genesis 8:7, it did not return "until the waters were dried up on face of the Earth," but we read on and find it never returned at all. We are told in Deuteronomy 34:6 that the burial place of Moses was not known "until the present day," but it still is not known. Here is a reference to a deuterocanonical book, 1 Maccabees. You don't accept it as inspired, but it shows usage of the word. 1 Maccabees 5:54: "And they went up to Mt. Sinai with joy and gladness because not one of them was slain until they had all returned in peace." It doesn't mean they were slain after they came home from the battle.

The word "until" in the Bible does not have the same meaning or implication it has today. Our natural implication is that if something didn't happen "until" now, then it will happen later. The Bible's use of the word does not imply that, as these verses show.

The other complaint is the term "firstborn." The firstborn is the child that opens the womb. Firstborn sons had to be sanctified, Exodus 34:20. There wasn't any reason to wait for a second son to come along before you could call the first one the firstborn. The first son you had was the firstborn from the moment of his birth. Archaeologists found in Egypt a funerary inscription which says, "This woman died giving birth to her firstborn son." Obviously he was her only son, so firstborn doesn't mean there were later-born children. Firstborn is a term of art because under the Jewish law there were certain responsibilities for the firstborn son.

So who were these brethren? Look at Matthew 27:56. Among them, at the cross, "were Mary Magdalene, and Mary the mother of James and Joseph, and the mother of the sons of Zebedee." Mark 15:40 says, "Among them were Mary Magdalene, and Mary the mother of James the less and of Joseph, and Salome." Compare those two to John 19:25, "Meanwhile his mother, and his mother's sister, Mary, the wife of Cleophas, and Mary Magdalene, had taken their stand beside the cross of Jesus."

If we compare those verses, we find that Mary, the mother of James and Joseph, must have been the wife of Cleophas, but James is elsewhere described as the son of Alphaeus. So does that mean this Mary, who is not the Virgin Mary, but a different Mary, was at once the wife of Cleophas and Alphaeus? There are two possibilities that scholars have mentioned. One, she could have been widowed and remarried, but more likely is that Alphaeus and Cleophas were the same person in that the Aramaic for Alphaeus could be rendered in

Greek as Cleophas. Just as Saul took another name, Paul, so Alphaeus also could be called, in Greek, Cleophas.

The early Christian writers, post-New Testament, speculated that this Cleophas was the brother of St. Joseph, the spouse of the Virgin Mary. Maybe, maybe not. If he was, then James would have been the cousin of Jesus. And in any case, there simply isn't anything in the New Testament which mandates that these people were brothers german to Jesus. So why, Catholics will ask, why do Fundamentalists bring this up? I'm surprised that nobody really brought it up earlier today.

I think there are two reasons: one is a dislike of celibacy in many quarters, the argument being that for Mary and Joseph to have been celibate would have been an unnatural family situation. It was unnatural anyway, having the Son of God in the family. Obviously this is a family which we cannot compare to any other family. It was established for a particular purpose, to nurture the Son of God.

The other reason is that I think some people hope to undermine respect for Mary by saying that basically she's like the rest of us. Furthermore, I think that a careful perusal of the New Testament will show that there isn't any indication there that she ever had other children. Certainly none of the early Christian writers ever suggested it. There is every indication that Jesus was her only child and that those called the brethren were his cousins. Thank you.

MODERATOR: Okay. I think we've about worn everybody out sufficiently. Let's stand and have a word of prayer, and we'll be dismissed.

# Thank You!

I hope you found this little book useful or entertaining—preferably both! If you did, please consider leaving an honest review at Amazon. It is through reviews that writers find most of their new readers.

If you have feedback about the book, I'd like to have it. You can write to me at Karl@KarlKeating.com.

# The Books in This Series

The Debating Catholicism Series consists of four short books and an omnibus volume. They are:

Book 1: *The Bible Battle* (Karl Keating vs. Peter S. Ruckman)

Book 2: *High Desert Showdown* (Karl Keating vs. Jim Blackburn)

Book 3: *Tracking Down the True Church* (Karl Keating vs. Jose Ventilacion)

Book 4: *Face Off with an Ex-Priest* (Karl Keating vs. Bartholomew F. Brewer)

Omnibus Volume: *Debating Catholicism* (includes all four books above)

# Other Books by Karl Keating

*Apologetics the English Way*

Can a reasonable case be made for Catholicism? Maybe even a compelling case? Or does the Catholic argument falter? Does it wilt before critiques from top-notch opponents? Judge for yourself. You don't have to be Catholic or even religious to relish the intellectual sparring that goes on in these pages.

Here is high-level controversial writing, culled from Karl Keating's favorite books. Each selection is a forceful exposition of Catholic truth. Most are from the 1930s, all come from English Catholics, and all are aimed at a single antagonist, with the public invited to look over the writer's shoulder. The reader can view the weaknesses and occasional mistakes even of his own champion.

These pages are filled with vivid personalities. These were men who knew the Catholic faith and could explain it to others. The individuals against whom they wrote may not have been converted—one or two were, in the long run—but any number of readers of these little-known masterpieces must have found their faith bolstered and their doubts assuaged. The issues covered in these exchanges are still discussed today—but probably nowhere in as glorious a style as here.

*The New Geocentrists*

Were Copernicus, Galileo, and Kepler wrong? Does Earth orbit the Sun, or does the Sun orbit Earth? For centuries, everyone thought the science was settled, but today the accepted cosmology is being challenged by writers, speakers, and movie producers who insist that science took a wrong turn in the seventeenth century. These new geocentrists claim not only that Earth is the center of our planetary system but that Earth is motionless at the very center of the universe.

They insist they have the science to back up their claims, which they buttress with evidence from the Bible and Church documents. But do they have a case? How solid is their reasoning, and how trustworthy are they as interpreters of science and theology?

*The New Geocentrists* examines the backgrounds, personalities, and arguments of the people involved in what they believe is a revolutionary movement, one that will overthrow the existing cosmological order and, as a consequence, change everyone's perception of the status of mankind.

## No Apology

Karl Keating has been a Catholic apologist for nearly four decades. In these pages he shares some of his own experiences and some stories from times past. He writes about how to do apologetics and how not to. He defends the very idea of apologetics against a theologian who thinks apologetics is passé. He looks at how the faith is promoted through beauty and through suffering. He takes you from his own backyard to such distant times and places as fifth-century Jerusalem and sixteenth-century Japan.

## Anti-Catholic Junk Food

You are what you eat. That is as true of the mind as of the body. Eat enough greasy food, and your silhouette will betray your culinary preferences. Give credence to enough greasy ideas, and your mind will be as flabby as your waistline. This book looks at eight examples of religious junk food, things that have come across Karl Keating's desk during his career as a Catholic apologist. You likely will find these morsels unconvincing and unpalatable, as you should. The problem is that plenty of people—including people on your block—consider such stuff to be intellectual high cuisine.

*Jeremiah's Lament*

For many, the best way to reach an understanding of the Catholic Church is to see how other people misunderstand it. This book is full of misunderstandings.

The people quoted in these pages came to their confusions in various ways. Sometimes it was by reading the wrong books or by failing to read the right books. Sometimes it was a matter of heredity, with prejudices passed down from father to son and from mother to daughter. At other times errors were imbibed at the foot of the pulpit, in the university lecture hall, or from door-to-door missionaries.

Whatever their origin, misunderstandings are misunderstandings. They should be recognized for what they are and set aside, even if that means a break from personal habit or family tradition. More than a century ago, Pope Leo XIII noted that there is nothing so salutary as to understand the world as it really is. That is true particularly of the Church that Christ established because to misunderstand her is to misunderstand him.

*How to Fail at Hiking Mt. Whitney*

Often, the best way to succeed at something is to learn how to fail at it—and then to avoid the things that lead to failure. There are books that tell you how to succeed at hiking Mt. Whitney. This book helps you *not* to fail by showing you what *not* to do, from the moment you start planning your trip to the moment you reach the summit.

You learn what gear not to buy and not to take, how to maximize your chances of getting a hiking permit (don't apply for the wrong days of the week!), how to prepare yourself physically without over-preparing, how to avoid being laid low by altitude or weather problems, how not to take too much food or water—or too little. You even discover how to shave a mile off the trip by using little-known shortcuts that can make the difference between reaching the summit and reaching exhaustion.

Most people who depart the Mt. Whitney trailhead fail to reach the top. Some fail because of things entirely beyond their control, but many fail because of insufficient preparation, false expectations, and basic errors of judgment. Their mistakes can come at the beginning (such as failing to get a hiking permit), during the preparation stage (such as being induced to buy "bombproof" gear), or during the hike (such as not heeding bodily warning signs).

Through engaging stories of his own and others' failures, Karl Keating shows you how to fail—and therefore how to succeed—at hiking the tallest peak in the 48 contiguous states.

# About Karl Keating

Karl Keating holds advanced degrees in theology and law (University of San Diego) plus an honorary doctor of laws degree (Ave Maria University). He founded Catholic Answers, the English-speaking world's largest lay-run Catholic apologetics organization. His best-known books are *Catholicism and Fundamentalism* (nearly a quarter-million paperback copies sold) and *What Catholics Really Believe* (about half that many sold). His avocations include hiking, studying languages, and playing the baroque mandolino. He lives in San Diego. You can follow him at his author website and on Facebook:

KarlKeating.com
Facebook.com/KarlKeatingBooks